Welcome to the wonderful world of crystals! Which one will be your favourite?

Aventurine

Wow! What a way to start our
crystal discovery!
This beautiful green crystal
is super super lucky!

Agate

This crystal comes in lots of different colours and has very pretty swirls. It will help you to concentrate.

Amazonite

Amazonite is the same colour as the ocean in the Caribbean. It is a helpful crystal and will help you to worry less and not be scared.

Amber

Amber looks like fire,
but is not as dangerous. It helps with
pain and can help take your
toothache away if you wear it as a
necklace.

Amethyst

This pretty purple crystal is very calming and will help you to have nice dreams if you put it near your bed.

Aquamarine

The stone of the sea,
it looks like the sea too!
Aquamarine is a stone of
courage and will help you
to be brave.

Azurite

Azurite will help open your magic third eye. It also helps with creativity, so keep it near you when you are making things!

Calcite

Calcite is a cleansing crystal. It can help with cleaning and clearing your magic energy field around you and your chakras.

Chalcedony

This crystal can help you with anxiety. So it can help you to stop worrying.

Charoite

Another pretty purple crystal. Charoite can help you get better quicker when you are sick.

Citrine

And another stone that looks like fire! But again, not as dangerous. Citrine can help your brain, keep it close to you when you need to do some work and use your brain lots.

Desert Rose

This can help your thinking and imagination.

Druzy

Druzy's come in all different colours. They can help you to achieve your goals. Tell your druzy what you want to achieve and it can help you.

Fluorite

Fluorite is pretty colours of purple, blues and greens. It can help bring clarity. So if you are confused about something, ask your Fluorite crystal to help you.

Howlite

This crystal can help you sleep and make your mind nice and calm.

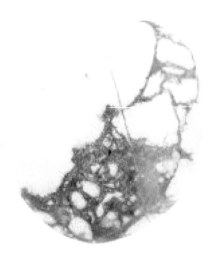

Idocrase

Idocrase, is a very rare crystal. Not many people have heard of this beautiful green crystal. It can help you to become a great inventor.

Jasper

Jasper comes in many different colours and can help you to feel happy and joyful!

Labradorite

This mesmerising crystal is good for self discovery, meaning it can help you to find out what you like and don't like.

Lapis Lazuli

When this crystal is polished into a round stone it looks like a magical blue planet with lots of lights. Just like labradorite it is a stone of self discovery, it is also a stone of peace. You can also mine this crystal in the game minecraft.

Larimar

A stone of relaxation, larimar can help you to have a calm and peaceful day.

Malachite

This is a protection stone. It absorbs negative energy, so can even help you to be a kinder person.

Moonstone

This is such a magical looking stone. It can help you with your emotions.

Obsidian

Obsidian is also a protection stone. If you have something new happening, like moving house or starting a new school, keep this stone near, it can help you to be excited instead of nervous.

Onyx

This stone is as black as the night! It can help you to have more self confidence.

Opal

Opal really is a magical crystal! It can help your psychic abilities.

Peridot

A happy and cheerful crystal. It can help you to get a nice sleep and bring good cheer and delight.

Phosphosiderite

This pretty purple stone is very rare. It can help you to be calm, and is good to use in meditation.

Pietersite

Pietersite is a variety of Quartz, composed naturally of Tiger's Eye, Hawk's Eye and Jasper. It can help you when you are nervous.

Prehnite

Prehnite is considered a stone of unconditional love. It can heal your heart and open it up to loving more.

Pyrite

Also called fools gold.
Pyrite can be your
personal bodyguard!
It is a very strong
protection stone.

Quartz

Quartz comes in lots of different colours and has a vast array of healing properties. Tell it your wishes to help them to come true.

Rhodonite

The stone of compassion. It can help you to heal from an argument and help you to stop panicking about a situation.

Sandstone

Sandstone can help you concentrate and improve your energy levels.

Tiger eye

This crystal can help you understand your feelings and situations.

Topaz

Topas can help to heal tummy pains and helps digestion.

Tourmaline

This crystal can help you when you need some inspiration.

Turquoise

These crystals can help your vocal cords. Wear it in a necklace if you want some help singing or speaking up.

Unakite

Encourages gratitude and can help you be thankful for the things you have.

Vanadinite

A very good supportive stone. Keep it near when you need a supporting hand to help you.

Printed in Great Britain
by Amazon